Which is the only mammal that can really fly?

a) an elephant ☐

b) a mouse ☐

c) a bat ☑

d) a squirrel ☐

1

From which part of a horse's body can you tell its age?

a) its tail ☐

b) its teeth ☐

c) its eyes ☐

d) its feet ☐

How long does it take the Earth to turn once on its axis?

a)   12 hours ☐

b)   2 hours ☐

c)   24 hours

d)   5 days ☐

If a dog barks and a cow moos, which creature gibbers?

a) an ape ☑

b) a goose ☐

c) a hamster ☐

d) a spider ☐

Where on a fly would you find its taste-buds?

a) tongue ☐
b) feet ☑
c) wings ☐
d) eyes ☐

Which word is spelt the same in English, French, Swedish and German?

a) hello

b) love

c) taxi

d) no

When toilet paper was first sold in 1857, what was printed on each side?

a) instructions ☐

b) a picture ☐

c) a name ☑

d) an address ☐

How can you make rubber bands last longer?

a) soak them ☐

b) dry them ☐

c) store them in a container ☐

d) put them in a fridge ☑

What is the name of the dot that we write on top of a small i?

a)   a tittle ☑

b)   an it ☐

c)   a whit ☐

d)   a tatt ☐

How long does it take an average person to fall asleep?

a) 5 minutes ☐

b) 7 minutes ☑

c) 10 minutes ☐

d) 14 minutes ☐

How many times can a woodpecker peck in a second?

a) 100 per second ☐

b) 50 per second ☐

c) 20 per second ☑

d) 10 per second ☐

Crossword puzzle

Across/Down answers filled in:

- 1. Benjamin
- 2. heavy
- 3. nails
- 4. cry
- 5. icecubes
- 6. cold

1. Ben is short for which boys name?

2. If something weighs a lot, it is....?

3. These are at the end of your fingers

4. You do this when you are sad

5. You put these in your drink to keep it cold

6. The opposite of hot

Word trail

Use the picture clues to fill in the word trail – the last letter of each word is the first of the next word.

What's gone wrong?

The artist has drawn some things wrongly in this picture.
Can you spot them?

Now showing....

MONKEYS IN THE FOG

TICKETS

coming so...

POP CORN

Puzzle wheel

Write the first letter of each picture in the space in the centre of the puzzle wheel. You will spell the name of an animal you may have as a pet.

Countries wordsearch

There are the names of 8 countries hidden in this wordsearch grid. Draw a ring around the words when you have found them.

C	A	N	A	D	A	R	T	E
H	Z	W	M	L	D	C	O	N
I	N	D	I	A	R	H	N	G
N	K	A	S	O	A	I	P	L
A	H	S	R	X	M	L	I	A
C	V	Y	A	N	K	E	D	N
G	R	E	E	C	E	E	S	D
P	E	K	L	J	T	L	F	I
D	C	S	E	Q	U	H	P	M
H	O	L	L	A	N	D	R	U

Hidden word

Cross out the letters that appear twice in the grid. Reading from top to bottom, the letters that are left spell the name of a country. Write your answer on the line below.

B	H	E	U	L
O	D	W	N	A
G	N	D	Y	W
A	Q	U	H	P
L	O	T	Q	B

Egypt

Word trail

Use the picture clues to fill in the word trail – the last letter of each word is the first of the next word.

Look and match

Look carefully at these signs. Which pictures do you think they go with? Draw lines to join the signs to the pictures.

SANDY BEACH

CHANGING ROOMS

PONY TREKKING

HAIRDRESSERS

What is the average body temperature of a dog?

a) 32°c

b) 40°c

c) 38.5°c

d) 37.2°c

The word 'pencil' once had a different meaning. What was it?

a) ink ☐

b) twig ☐

c) brush ☑

d) apple ☐

Which bird was called 'the peacock of the Indies' when it was first discovered?

a) an eagle

b) a chicken

c) a turkey

d) a dodo

In Morse code which letter is shown by a single dot or flash?

a) z ☐

b) s ☐

c) a ☐

d) e ☐

Which swimming stroke is named after an insect?

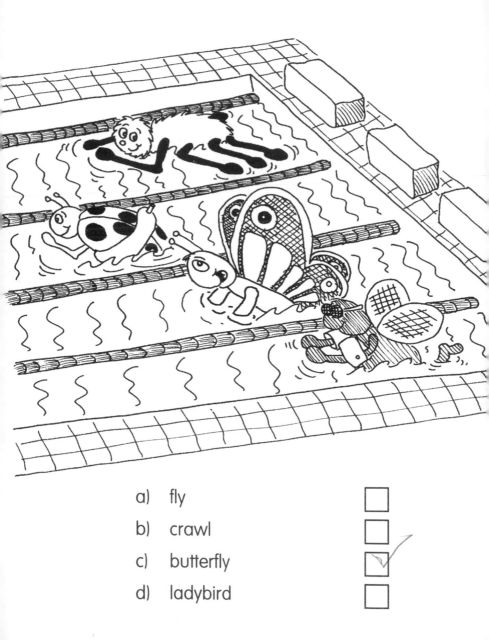

a) fly ☐

b) crawl ☐

c) butterfly ☑

d) ladybird ☐

Which units are used to measure a horse?

a) metres ☐

b) hands ☐

c) legs ☐

d) litres ☐

What is a female deer called?

a) a doe ☑

b) Mary ☐

c) a stag ☐

d) a foal ☐

What is the only bird that can hover in the air and fly backwards?

a) a hummingbird ✔

b) an eagle ☐

c) a sparrow ☐

d) a chicken ☐

How many stomachs does a cow have?

a) 2

b) 9

c) 4 ✓

d) 1

What is the opening at the top of a volcano called?

a) a crater ☑

b) a hole ☐

c) a crust ☐

d) a dip ☐

How many legs does an octopus have?

a) 2

b) 4

c) 5

d) 8

Crossword puzzle

1. This person travels in space
2. Use this to wash your hair
3. The hair on a man's chin
4. The opposite of thin
5. The hottest season of the year
6. You wash with this

Fishy tale

Follow the lines to connect the fishermen to their catch.
Which fisherman has caught the biggest fish?

Puzzle wheel

Write the first letter of each picture in the space in the centre of the puzzle wheel. You will spell the name of a fish.

Word trail

Use the picture clues to fill in the word trail – the last letter of each word is the first of the next word.

Where in the world?

There are the names of 8 countries hidden in this wordsearch grid. Draw a ring around the words when you have found them.

M	E	X	I	C	O	X	S	J
A	D	F	L	M	B	I	O	A
L	Z	I	T	A	L	Y	X	P
A	G	Y	V	G	H	A	N	A
Y	J	F	P	K	A	I	W	N
S	H	T	C	R	Z	Q	I	Q
I	R	E	L	A	N	D	U	P
A	R	D	K	M	X	H	G	E
J	K	C	T	U	P	U	I	R
T	U	R	K	E	Y	E	M	U

Puzzle wheel

Write the first letter of each picture in the space in the centre of the puzzle wheel. You will spell the name of a country.

Jumble

Unscramble these anagrams to make new words.
The pictures are clues. Write the words on the lines.

epolteneh	kornigc arihc

_____

danlec	lisrequr

_____

Which part of its body does a snake use to listen?

a) tongue ☐

b) eyes ☐

c) tail ☐

d) teeth ☐

How many teeth does an adult have?

a) 22

b) 32

c) 42

d) 52

What are penguins covered in?

a) feathers

b) fur

c) scales

d) rubber

Which animal has the longest life span?

a) an elephant ☐

b) a giant tortoise ☐

c) a donkey ☐

d) a crocodile ☐

What is the average number of fleas found on a hedgehog?

a) 500

b) 100

c) 50

d) 20

Which is the largest creature ever to have lived on earth?

a) tyrannosaurus rex ☐

b) blue whale ☑

c) elephant ☐

d) walrus ☐

What type of dance involves moving under a low horizontal pole?

a) a waltz ☐

b) a limbo ☑

c) the twist ☐

d) the pogo ☐

Where does a kangaroo keep its young?

a)   in its pouch   ✓

b)   in a nest

c)   on its back

d)   in a tree

Why do wolves howl?

a) to scare other animals ☐

b) to start a fight ☐

c) to announce the full moon ☐

d) to tell other wolves where they are ☑

What does a scorpion have at the end of its tail?

a) taste buds ☐

b) eyes ☐

c) sting ☑

d) hairs ☐

What does a chameleon change to hide itself from predators?

a) its colour

b) its tail

c) its fur

d) its home

Puzzle wheel

Write the first letter of each picture in the space in the centre of the puzzle wheel. You will spell the name of an animal.

Gardening

Which of these things can be used when doing the gardening? Put ticks in the boxes.

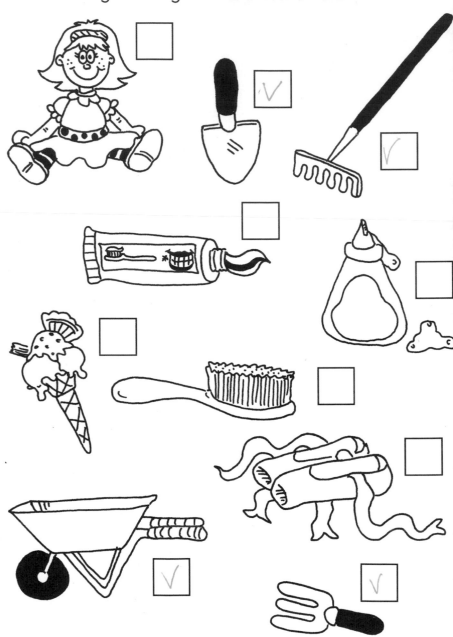

What's gone wrong?

The artist has drawn some things wrongly in this picture.
Can you spot them?

Puzzle wheel

Write the first letter of each picture in the space in the centre of the puzzle wheel. You will spell the name of a planet.

Hidden word

Cross out the letters that appear twice in the grid.
Reading from top to bottom, the letters that are left
spell the name of a sea creature. Write your answer
on the line below.

J	E	D	T	O
K	L	G	R	P
U	R	H	J	G
I	M	A	U	K
T	E	A	M	N

Dolphin

Word trail

Use the picture clues to fill in the word trail – the last letter of each word is the first of the next word.

Plant spotting

There are the names of 8 flowers and plants hidden in this wordsearch grid. Draw a ring around the words when you have found them.

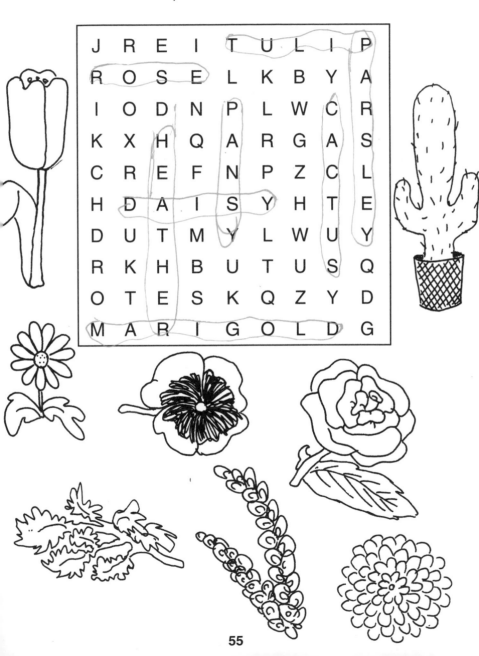

J	R	E	I	T	U	L	I	P
R	O	S	E	L	K	B	Y	A
I	O	D	N	P	L	W	C	R
K	X	H	Q	A	R	G	A	S
C	R	E	F	N	P	Z	C	L
H	D	A	I	S	Y	H	T	E
D	U	T	M	Y	L	W	U	Y
R	K	H	B	U	T	U	S	Q
O	T	E	S	K	Q	Z	Y	D
M	A	R	I	G	O	L	D	G

Jumble

Unscramble these anagrams to make new words.
The pictures are clues. Write the words on the lines.

rief ecalp	nacdocori

_____

_____

eganmobor	ogtsh

_____

_____

How many colours are there in a rainbow?

a) 5

b) 3

c) 8

d) 7 ✔

Which event did the first popular greeting card celebrate?

a) Christmas ☐

b) Valentine's Day ☐

c) Easter ☐

d) Mother's Day ☐

What is the tail of a red fox called?

a) a whoosh ☐

b) a broom ☐

c) a brush ☐

d) a bush ☑

In which country is the kimono the national dress for women?

a) Japan ☐

b) China ☐

c) Spain ☐

d) Australia ☐

What part of a golden eagle is gold?

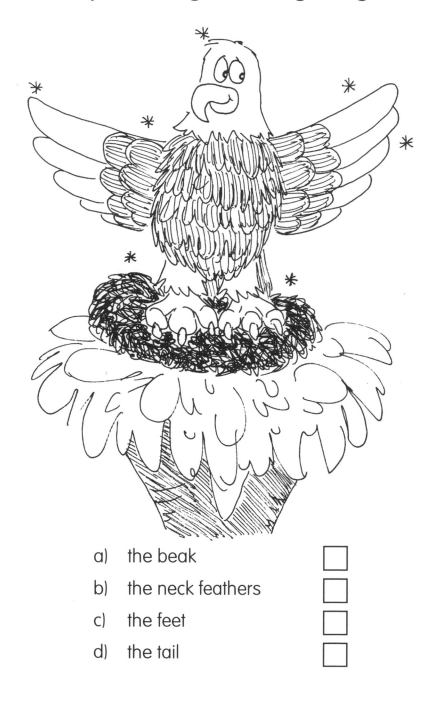

a) the beak ☐
b) the neck feathers ☐
c) the feet ☐
d) the tail ☐

Which is the largest bird in the world?

a) a goose ☐

b) a vulture ☐

c) an ostrich ☑

d) an eagle owl ☐

What is the national flower of Austria?

a) edelweiss ☐

b) daisy ☐

c) rose ☐

d) tulip ☐

What are pigs' feet called?

a) hooves

b) trotters

c) paws

d) claws

From which country did the Hamburger originate?

a) United States of America ☐

b) England ☐

c) France ☐

d) Germany ☐

What 'colour' is the Sea between Egypt and Saudi Arabia?

a) black

b) pink

c) green

d) red

What is the hyena well-known for?

a) laughing ☑

b) dribbling ☐

c) walking backwards ☐

d) hissing ☐

On the beach

Two people in this picture are going to play a game of tennis, can you find them both?

What's gone wrong?

The artist has drawn some things wrongly in this picture.
Can you spot them?

Puzzle wheel

Write the first letter of each picture in the space in the centre of the puzzle wheel. You will spell the name of a colour.

Clothes wordsearch

There are the names of 8 types of clothes hidden in this wordsearch grid. Draw a ring around the words when you have found them.

```
G  K  I  J  U  M  P  E  R
S  R  O  X  U  K  M  D  O
H  A  T  G  S  O  C  K  S
I  M  W  P  H  I  V  Z  A
R  F  B  M  O  N  O  P  D
T  E  I  Z  E  X  H  O  D
A  L  L  T  S  U  S  S  R
E  D  Y  I  Q  E  T  I  E
H  O  Z  C  M  Q  U  P  S
S  T  R  O  U  S  E  R  S
```

Hidden word

Cross out the letters that appear twice in the grid.
Reading from top to bottom, the letters that are left spell
a boy's name. Write your answer on the line below.

D	J	I	Z	W
T	G	U	Q	A
M	Q	O	E	H
H	O	G	D	T
I	W	Z	S	U

Word trail

Use the picture clues to fill in the word trail – the last letter of each word is the first of the next word.

Puzzle wheel

Write the first letter of each picture in the space in the centre of the puzzle wheel. You will spell a boy's name.

In which country is Table Mountain?

a) Spain ☐

b) Australia ☐

c) Holland ☐

d) South Africa ☐

What type of fish are threshers and hammerheads?

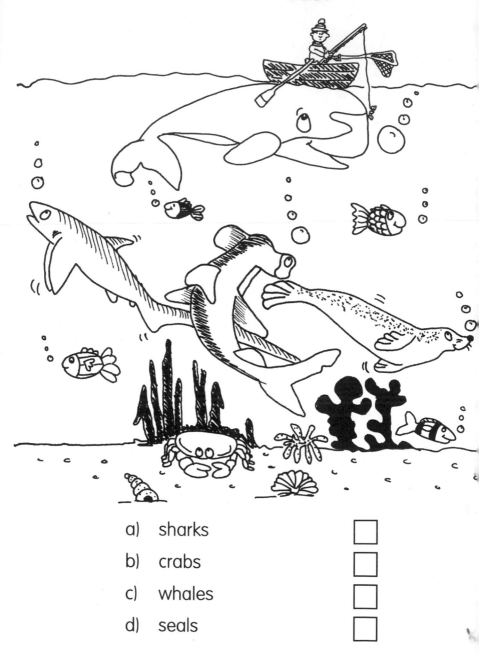

a) sharks ☐

b) crabs ☐

c) whales ☐

d) seals ☐

What type of insect is a 'painted lady'?

a) a ladybird

b) a butterfly

c) a spider

d) a wasp

Which is the fastest land animal?

a) a horse ☐

b) a cheetah ☐

c) a puma ☐

d) a tortoise ☐

Which is the largest of the cat family?

a) a puma ☐

b) a panther ☐

c) a leopard ☐

d) a tiger ☐

How many sets of teeth do most mammals have?

a) 3 ☐

b) 2 ☐

c) 6 ☐

d) 1 ☐

What do beavers build?

a) dams ☑

b) nests ☐

c) bridges ☐

d) towers ☐

What does a sculptor do?

a) draw pictures ☐

b) make statues ☑

c) look after animals ☐

d) build roads ☐

How many points are there on a snowflake?

a) 4

b) 6

c) 3

d) 14

How many ribs does a human have?

a) 12

b) 18

c) 24

d) 32

Which planet is nearest to the sun?

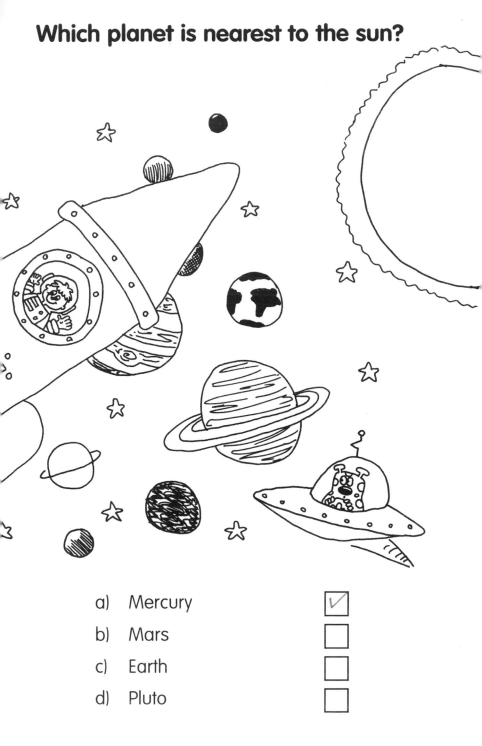

a) Mercury   ☑

b) Mars   ☐

c) Earth   ☐

d) Pluto   ☐

Hidden rabbits

Can you find 6 baby rabbits hidden in this picture?
They are hiding from the mother rabbit.

What's gone wrong?

The artist has drawn some things wrongly in this picture.
Can you spot them?

Puzzle wheel

Write the first letter of each picture in the space in the centre of the puzzle wheel. You will spell a girl's name.

Questions and answers

The answers to these questions can be found in the boxes. Draw a line to match the questions to the answers.

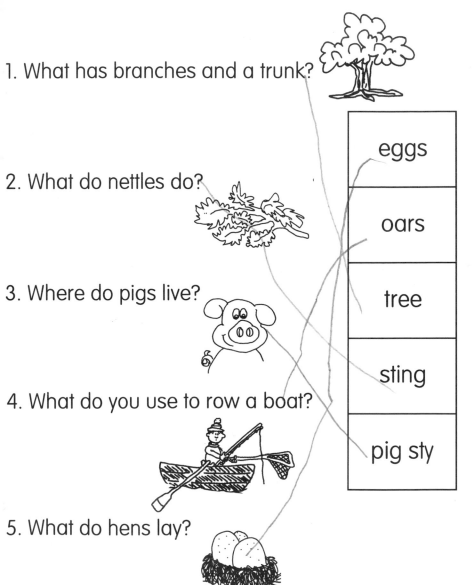

1. What has branches and a trunk?

2. What do nettles do?

3. Where do pigs live?

4. What do you use to row a boat?

5. What do hens lay?

eggs

oars

tree

sting

pig sty

Hidden word

Cross out the letters that appear twice in the grid.
Reading from top to bottom, the letters that are left spell
a girl's name. Write your answer on the line below.

W	J	T	O	Z
G	B	P	U	F
L	Y	G	B	Y
O	Z	F	N	I
P	N	A	T	W

_____

Word trail

Use the picture clues to fill in the word trail – the last
letter of each word is the first of the next word.

Puzzle wheel

Write the first letter of each picture in the space in the centre of the puzzle wheel. You will spell the name of a tree.

Jumble

Unscramble these anagrams to make new words.
The pictures are clues. Write the words on the lines.

rebcige

eehhggdo

_____

_____

mihyecn

dastlooto

_____

_____

In what country were fireworks invented?

a) Italy ☐

b) China ☐

c) Australia ☐

d) England ☐

How does a squid defend itself?

a) by making a loud noise ☐

b) by squirting ink ☐

c) by hiding in seaweed ☐

d) by turning red ☐

Which bird lays the largest eggs?

a) an emu ☐

b) an ostrich ☐

c) a golden eagle ☐

d) a turkey ☐

Which insects communicate with one another by dancing?

a) butterflies ☐

b) spiders ☐

c) bees ☐

d) ladybirds ☐

How often are the Olympic Games held?

a) once a year ☐

b) every 2 years ☐

c) every 4 years ☐

d) every 6 years ☐

Which fruit becomes a prune when it is dried?

a) a grape ☐

b) a pineapple ☐

c) a lemon ☐

d) a plum ☐

What do you call a group of fish?

a) a tribe ☐

b) a shoal ☑

c) a pride ☐

d) a wibble ☐

Why are parrots so brightly coloured?

a)   as a warning to other birds ☐

b)   to attract other parrots ☐

c)   as camouflage ☐

d)   to show off ☐

What does a caterpillar turn into when it becomes an adult?

a) a ladybird ☐

b) a spider ☑

c) a butterfly ☐

d) a frog ☐

What is a rabbit's underground home called?

a) a stable ☐

b) a burrow ☑

c) a den ☐

d) a tunnel ☐

Which of your senses are you using when you listen to music?

a) hearing ☑
b) sight ☐
c) taste ☐
d) smell ☐

Crossword puzzle

1. This helps you to work out sums
2. A long, thin orange vegetable
3. Keeps you dry in the rain
4. You go to sleep in one of these
5. An eskimo lives in this
6. This plant has red berries and green pointed leaves

Jigsaw puzzle

Can you see the jigsaw pieces that go together? Draw lines to join them.

What's gone wrong?

The artist has drawn some things wrongly in this picture.
Can you spot them?

Puzzle wheel

Write the first letter of each picture in the space in the centre of the puzzle wheel. You will spell the name of a fruit.

Questions and answers

The answers to these questions can be found in the boxes. Draw a line to match the questions to the answers.

What is the opposite of heavy?

. What appears during the sun and rain?

. What does a jockey ride?

. What grows in a paddy field?

. What do astronauts travel in?

horse
rice
light
space shuttle
rainbow

Hidden word

Cross out the letters that appear twice in the grid. Reading from top to bottom, the letters that are left spell the name of a tree. Write your answer on the line below.

D	U	N	F	Q
B	O	C	I	M
R	C	D	L	A
U	Q	I	M	R
N	F	K	L	B

Word trail

Use the picture clues to fill in the word trail – the last letter of each word is the first of the next word.

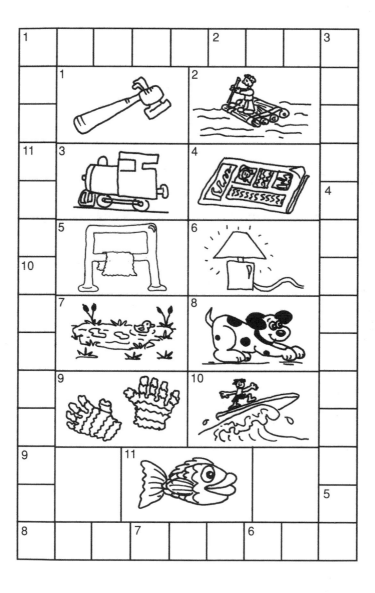

Jumble

Unscramble these anagrams to make new words.
The pictures are clues. Write the words on the lines.

trewa ylli	rrottca

_____   _____

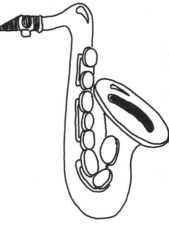

asdewee	nooxashep

_____   _____

In which country would you find pyramids and sphinxes?

a) Australia ☐

b) Egypt ☑

c) India ☐

d) France ☐

In which country do kangaroos and koalas live?

a) America ☐

b) Russia ☐

c) Australia ☐

d) China ☐

How many sides are there to a hexagon?

a) 8

b) 6

c) 4

d) 2

What is the boiling point of water?

a) 50°c ☐

b) 75°c ☐

c) 100°c ☐

d) 200°c ☐

In which month is Valentine's Day?

a) January ☐

b) February ☐

c) November ☐

d) December ☐

In which country is the Eiffel tower?

a) France ☑
b) Germany ☐
c) Spain ☐
d) Africa ☐

How many legs has a spider?

a) 4 ☐
b) 6 ☐
c) 8 ☐
d) 10 ☐

In which country would you find the Statue of Liberty?

a) Australia ☐

b) United States of America ☐

c) England ☐

d) Norway ☐

At what temperature does water freeze?

a) 0°c ☐

b) 15°c ☐

c) -50°c ☐

d) -75°c ☐

Which animal's name means river horse?

a) crocodile ☐

b) elephant ☐

c) hippopotamus ☑

d) zebra ☐

What edible sugary substance do bees make?

a) jam ☐

b) marmalade ☐

c) lemon curd ☐

d) honey ☑

What's gone wrong?

The artist has drawn some things wrongly in this picture. Can you spot them?

Puzzle wheel

Write the first letter of each picture in the space in the centre of the puzzle wheel. You will spell the name of a colour and a fruit.

Questions and answers

The answers to these questions can be found in the boxes. Draw a line to match the questions to the answers.

1. What is the top room in a house?

2. What is the day after today?

3. What do you spread on bread?

4. What is another word for donkey?

5. What do chefs do?

cook
ass
tomorrow
attic
butter

Word trail

Use the picture clues to fill in the word trail – the last letter of each word is the first of the next word.

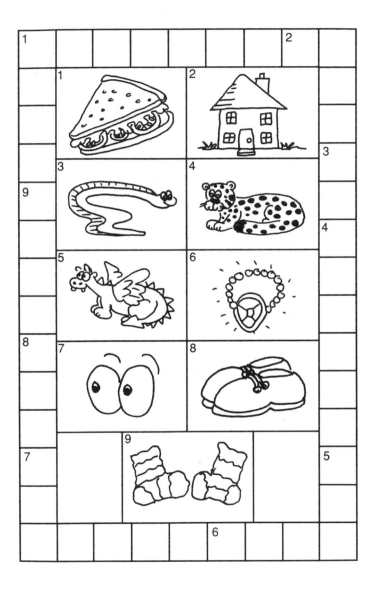

Questions and answers

The answers to these questions can be found in the boxes. Draw a line to match the questions to the answers.

1. What kind of pet barks?

2. What appears in the sky at night?

3. What is a female goat called?

4. What is the opposite of bottom?

| nanny |
| wine |
| top |
| stars |
| dog |

5. What drink are grapes made into?

Pet spotting

There are the names of 8 pets hidden in this wordsearch grid. Draw a ring around the words when you have found them.

R	B	C	A	N	A	R	Y	S
A	W	A	Q	Y	G	J	F	B
B	I	T	A	M	O	U	S	E
B	R	D	C	S	L	K	L	E
I	R	W	V	Z	D	O	G	V
T	H	L	J	S	F	T	O	D
Q	Y	R	B	C	I	D	X	P
U	B	H	A	M	S	T	E	R
H	V	M	T	S	H	S	O	A
P	O	N	Y	E	Y	E	O	M

Puzzle wheel

Write the first letter of each picture in the space in the centre of the puzzle wheel. You will spell the name of some clothing.

Jumble

Unscramble these anagrams to make new words.
The pictures are clues. Write the words on the lines.

| l o d l' s   e s h u o | | l u s r a w |

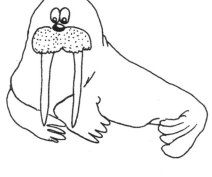

| h i f e l s j l y | | c e t o s o r |

Which Australian bird does not fly?

a) an emu ☐

b) a kookaburra ☐

c) a macaw ☐

d) a sparrow ☐

Which group of birds is called a 'gaggle'?

a) swallows ☐
b) geese ☐
c) turkeys ☐
d) crows ☐

How much blood is there in an average human?

a) 10 gallons ☐

b) 2 wines ☐

c) 8 pints ☐

d) 5 pints ☐

What is a female swan called?

a) a hen ☐

b) a pen ☐

c) a pencil ☐

d) a cobb ☐

What is the front of a boat called?

a) the back ☐

b) the port ☐

c) the bow ☐

d) the point ☐

What is a baby horse called?

a) a filly ☐

b) a mare ☐

c) a foal ☐

d) a calf ☐

Which animal is often called the 'ship of the desert'?

a) a horse ☐

b) a camel ☐

c) an elephant ☐

d) a tiger ☐

What is the name for animals that come out only at night?

a) nocturnal ☐
b) short-sighted ☐
c) hunters ☐
d) visible ☐

Where would you find an oasis?

a) on a beach ☐

b) up a mountain ☐

c) under the sea ☐

d) in a desert ☐

What do some animals do between winter and spring?

a) go skiing ☐

b) put their warm coats on ☐

c) hibernate ☐

d) play golf ☐

How many days are there in a year?

a) 300 ☐

b) 365 ☐

c) 375 ☐

d) 395 ☐

A royal mess!

The King has lost his crown! Look carefully at this picture. Can you spot it?

Puzzle wheel

Write the first letter of each picture in the space in the centre of the puzzle wheel. You will spell the name of a woodland animal.

Questions and answers

The answers to these questions can be found in the boxes. Draw a line to match the questions to the answers.

1. What colour usually means stop?

2. What does a shepherd look after?

3. What is the first meal of the day?

| breakfast |
| purr |
| snail |
| red |
| sheep |

4. What noise do cats make?

5. Which creature carries its home on its back?

Word trail

Use the picture clues to fill in the word trail – the last letter of each word is the first of the next word.

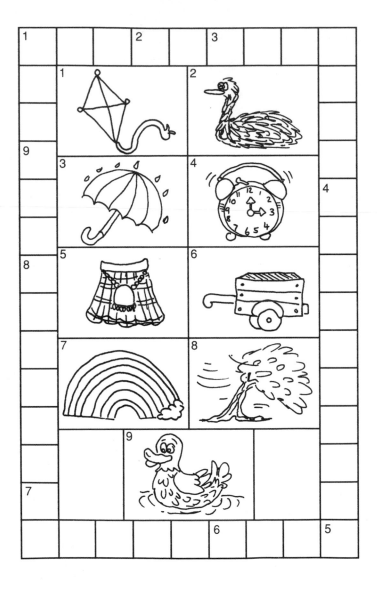

Jumble

Unscramble these anagrams to make new words.
The pictures are clues. Write the words on the lines.

s e p i l s p r	f s u r a o b d r

_____

_____

t e f l y u b t r	a a r m l c c o k l

_____

_____

Puzzle wheel

Write the first letter of each picture in the space in the centre of the puzzle wheel. You will spell the name of some flowers.

Crossword puzzle

1. A skeleton is made of these
2. This flower has thorns
3. Not brother but . . .
4. Cars run on this fuel
5. Tell the time with this
6. These shine in the sky at night

Word trail

Use the picture clues to fill in the word trail – the last letter of each word is the first of the next word.

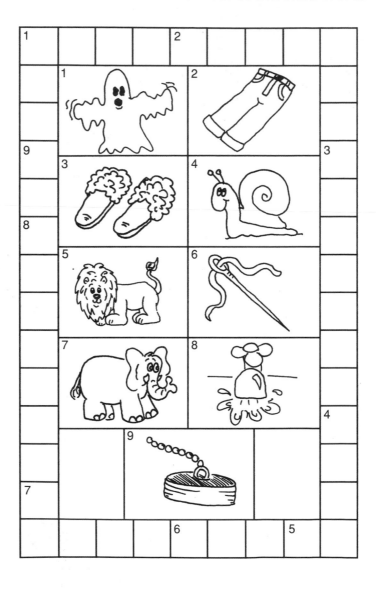

Fancy dress

These two pictures of children in fancy dress look the same but there are 8 differences to find in the second picture.

Walking the dog

Follow the lines to find out which dog each child is taking for a walk.

Answers

1 c) a bat
2 b) its teeth
3 c) 24 hours
4 a) an ape
5 b) feet
6 c) taxi
7 c) a name
8 d) put them in a fridge
9 a) a tittle
10 b) 7 minutes
11 c) 20 per second

12 **Crossword puzzle**

```
      ²h        ³n
  ¹B e n j a m ⁵i n
      a       i   c
      v       l   e
  ⁴c r y      s  ⁶c o l d
                  u
                  b
                  e
                  s
```

13 **Word trail**
1 ear
2 ring
3 grapes
4 snowman
5 nest
6 teapot
7 tail
8 lamp
9 panda
10 acorn
11 nurse

14 **What's gone wrong?**
1 bus stop sign
2 snake on ticket booth
3 paw prints
4 girl selling popcorn
   wearing jesters hat
5 girl wearing ice skates

15 **Puzzle wheel**
rabbit

16 **Countries wordsearch**

```
C A N A D A R T E
H Z W M L D C O N
I N D I A R H N G
N K A S O A I P L
A H S R X M L I A
C V Y A N K E D N
G R E E C E S D
P E K L J T L F I
D C S E Q U H P M
H O L L A N D R U
```

17 **Hidden word**
EGYPT

18 **Word trail**
1 elephant
2 top
3 parrot
4 train
5 nail
6 leaf
7 feather
8 rabbit
9 tree
10 eagle

19 Look and Match
pony trekking – saddle
sandy beach – bucket and spade
changing rooms – shirt
hairdressers – scissors and comb

20 c) 38.5°c
21 c) brush
22 c) a turkey
23 d) e
24 c) butterfly
25 b) hands
26 a) a doe
27 a) a hummingbird
28 c) 4
29 a) a crater
30 d) 8

31 Crossword puzzle

			³b		⁴f
			e		a
¹a	²s	t	r	o	n	a	u	t
	h				r
	a				d
⁵s	u	m	m	e	r
	p		
	o		
⁶s	o	a	p

32 Fishy tale
The fisherman in the middle

33 Puzzle wheel
salmon

34 Word trail
1 dolphin
2 net
3 telephone
4 egg
5 goat
6 television
7 nest
8 teacher
9 road

35 Where in the world?

36 Puzzle wheel
Brazil

37 Jumble
telephone
rocking chair
candle
squirrel

38 a) tongue
39 b) 32
40 a) feathers
41 b) a giant tortoise
42 a) 500
43 b) blue whale
44 b) a limbo
45 a) in its pouch
46 d) to tell other wolves
    where they are
47 c) sting
48 a) its colour

49 **Puzzle wheel**
    donkey

50 **Gardening**
    trowel
    rake
    wheel barrow
    fork

51 **What's gone wrong?**
    1 elephant in crowd
    2 pineapple on ring
      master's head
    3 wheels on skateboard
      missing
    4 clown has fish instead
      of bow tie
    5 unicyclist one shoe
      missing

52 **Puzzle wheel**
    Saturn

53 **Hidden word**
    DOLPHIN

54 **Word trail**
    1 shop
    2 panda
    3 ant
    4 toy
    5 yo-yo
    6 ostrich
    7 hospital
    8 lighthouse
    9 ear
    10 rings

55 **Plant spotting**

J	R	E	I	T	U	L	I	P
R	O	S	E	L	K	B	Y	A
I	O	D	N	P	L	W	C	R
K	X	H	Q	A	R	G	A	S
C	R	E	F	N	P	Z	C	L
H	D	A	I	S	Y	H	T	E
D	U	T	M	Y	L	W	U	Y
R	K	H	B	U	T	U	S	Q
O	T	E	S	K	Q	Z	Y	D
M	A	R	I	G	O	L	D	G

56 **Jumble**
    fire place
    accordion
    boomerang
    ghost

57 d) 7
58 b) Valentine's Day
59 c) a brush
60 a) Japan
61 b) the neck feathers
62 c) an ostrich
63 a) edelweiss
64 b) trotters
65 d) Germany
66 d) red
67 a) laughing

69 **What's gone wrong?**
1 cat sitting at table
2 a kite flying
3 a sock on the table
4 bird on clown's head
5 snails on table

70 **Puzzle wheel**
violet

71 **Clothes wordsearch**

72 **Hidden word**
JAMES

73 **Word trail**
1 ghost
2 tractor
3 rollerboot
4 tomato
5 octopus
6 snail
7 leopard
8 dog

74 **Puzzle wheel**
Thomas

75 d) South Africa
76 a) sharks
77 b) a butterfly
78 b) a cheetah
79 d) a tiger
80 b) 2 but not at the
same time!
81 a) dams
82 b) make statues
83 b) 6
84 c) 24
85 a) Mercury

87 **What's gone wrong?**
1 end of swings missing
2 boy on swing
wearing skis
3 stars in the daytime
4 boy wearing saucepan
on his head
5 a giraffe in the hedge

		⁵i							²c
		g							a
¹c	a	l	c	³u	l	a	t	o	r
		o		m					r
		o		⁴b	e	d			o
				r					t
				e					
		⁶h	o	l	l	y			
				l					
				a					

109 **Questions and answers**
1 light
2 rainbow
3 horse
4 rice
5 space shuttle

110 **Hidden word**
OAK

111 **Word trail**
1 hammer
2 raft
3 train
4 newspaper
5 rail
6 lamp
7 pond
8 dog
9 gloves
10 surf
11 fish

112 **Jumble**
water lily
tractor
seaweed
saxophone

113 b) Egypt
114 c) Australia
115 b) 6
116 c) 100°c
117 b) February

118 a) France
119 c) 8
120 b) United States
of America
121 a) 0°c
122 c) hippopotamus
123 d) honey

124 **What's gone wrong?**
1 deer wearing hat
2 flying mouse
3 pencil instead of tree
trunk
4 mole wearing sun
glasses
5 chimney

125 **Puzzle wheel**
orange

126 **Questions and answers**
1 attic
2 tomorrow
3 butter
4 ass
5 cook

127 **Word trail**
1 sandwich
2 house
3 eel
4 leopard
5 dragon
6 necklace

7 eyes
8 shoes
9 socks

128 **Questions and answers**
1 dog
2 stars
3 nanny
4 top
5 wine

129 **Pet spotting**

130 **Puzzle wheel**
jumper

131 **Jumble**
doll's house
walrus
jellyfish
scooter

132 a) an emu
133 b) geese
134 c) 8 pints
135 b) a pen
136 c) the bow
137 c) a foal

138 b) a camel
139 a) nocturnal
140 d) in a desert
141 c) hibernate
142 b) 365

144 **Puzzle wheel**
badger

145 **Questions and answers**
1 red
2 sheep
3 breakfast
4 purr
5 snail

146 **Word trail**
1 kite
2 emu
3 umbrella
4 alarm clock
5 kilt
6 trailer
7 rainbow
8 wind
9 duck

147 **Jumble**
slippers
surf board
butterfly
alarm clock

148 Puzzle wheel
tulips

149 Crossword puzzle

```
        ¹b
  ²r  o  s  e        ⁶s
        n     ⁴p     t
        e     e      a
       ³s  i  s  t  e  r
              r      s
              o
          ⁵c  l  o  c  k
```

150 Word trail
1 ghost
2 trousers
3 slippers
4 snail
5 lion
6 needle
7 elephant
8 tap
9 plug

151 Fancy dress
1 hat on dog missing
2 feather in cowboy's hat
3 flower on cowboy's waistcoat
4 pattern on the witch's hat
5 witch's hair
6 jester's hat
7 jester's trousers
8 jester's shoes